Farm
Babies

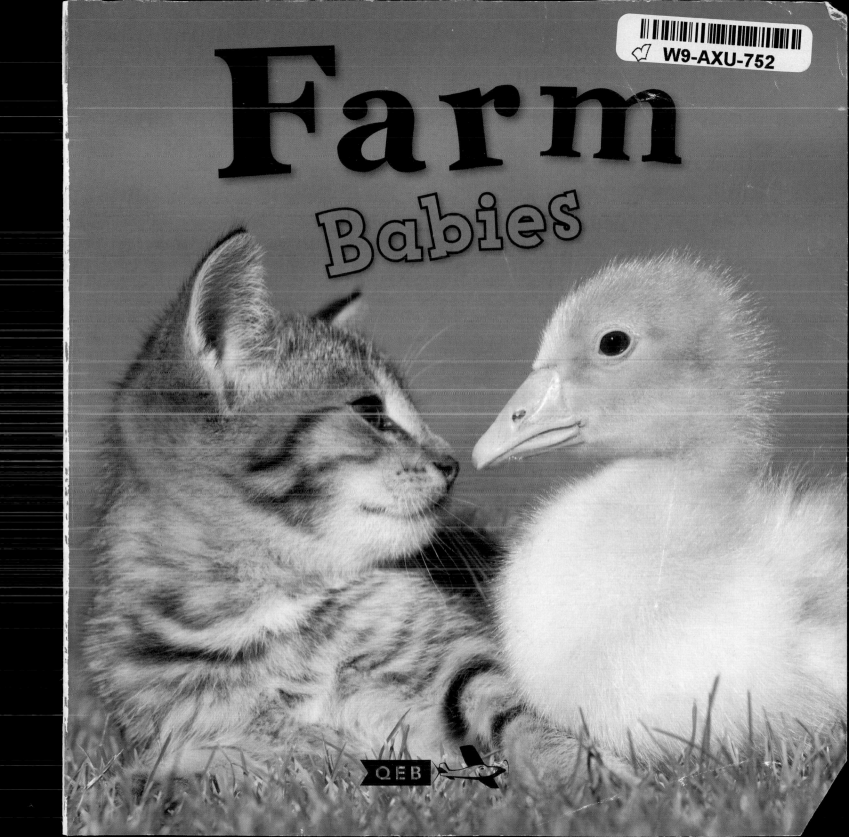

QEB

Quarto is the authority on a wide range of topics.

Quarto educates, entertains and enriches the lives of our readers—enthusiasts and lovers of hands-on living.

www.quartoknows.com

Copyright © QEB Publishing, Inc. 2016

First published in the United States in 2016
by QEB Publishing, Inc.
Part of The Quarto Group
6 Orchard
Lake Forest, CA 92630

Designer: Tracy Killick Art Direction & Design
Editor: Joanna McInerney
Picture Researcher: Jen Veall

A CIP record for this book is available from the Library of Congress.

ISBN 978 1 68297 130 7

Printed in China

PICTURE CREDITS
a=above, c=centre, b=bottom, l=left, r=right

123RF Andrew Mayovskyy 28; Ilya Karnaukhov 48 b; marcogovel 56 bl; Natalia Matveeva 19 al; Ratchapol Yindeesuk 52 b; Roman Pyshchyk 15 br; Tracey Helmboldt 10 b; yoshiyayo 44 al

Alamy Stock Photo Burghard Schreyer 56 br; Duncan Usher 15 a; Foto Grebler 13 b; guy harrop 62; Herbert Spichtinger/Image Source 1; imageBROKER 21 al; Mark J. Barrett 63 bl; Peter Cripps 63 br; Reg Pengelly 47; Vanessa Grossemy 8 ar

Dreamstime.com 400ex127 53; Andrey Puhash 11; Brett Critchley 24; Bronwyn8 43 b; Carola Schubbel 29 b; Daniel Wiedemann 21 ar; Dennis Van De Water 51 bl; Dianazh 45 a; Geza Farkas 32 ar; Goce Risteski 18 br; Goncharuk Maksym 25 br; Larry Metayer 34 br; Lifeontheside 34 bl; Loshadenok 32 al; Mark Graham 34 a; Maximilian Pogonii 26 ar; Mysikrysa 26 al; Nailia

Schwarz 54 bl; Pavel Mozzhukhin 64; Renewillms 49 br; Robert Mawby 20; Robhainer 60; Snowboy234 48 a

FLPA Ramona Richter/Tierfotoagentur 30 bl, 30 bc, 30-31 b, 31 bc, 31 br

Getty Images Christian Paoli 41 bl; Steven Kazlowski 39 al

iStockphoto anopdesignstock 5 al; Daniel MAR 16 br; DHuss 58 br, 59 al; eli_asenova 45 b; Gord Horne 59 b; nomis_g 54 br; Oliver Malms 13 al; oscarshost 46 br; Pierre Cardon 61 br; pjmalsbury 54 ar; predrag1 19 br; Rico Domonkos 6 br, 7 bl, 7 br; Serega 61 bl; tvirbickis 41 br

Shutterstock aaltair 37 br; Africa Studio 51 br; Alexandr Andreiko 27 r; Amy Johansson 21 b; andia 25 a; anetapics 8 br; belizar 46 ar; bogdanhoda 37 bl; Bozhena Melnyk 6 a; Brittarose 27 bl; Catalin Petolea 25 bl; cellistka 39 bl; cgdeaw 22 al; Cornelia Anghel 23; cowboy54 56 al; DragoNika 30 ar; Drew Horne 56 ar; eastern light

photography 32 bl; Eric Gevaert 2-3, 36; Flipser 54 al; Galyna Andrushko 57; GeNik 41 a; Howard Klaaste 49 bl; irin-k 50; jdm.foto 40; Jiang Hongyan 5 r, 14 l; Jiri Hera 8 l; JLSnader 10 a; Joseph C. Salonis 5 bl; Juan He 43 ar; lantapix chick silhouette artwork throughout; Lindsay Helms 58 l; lostbear 22 b; Lynne Carpenter 26 b; mariait 12 a; marilyn barbone 37 a; Martin Mecnarowski 52 a; Montenegro 16 a; Mykola Kindzerskyi 14 r; Nate Allred 42; NikkiHoff 7 al; Noppharat4569 43 al; Oleksii Zelivianskyi 16 bl; Olga_i 12 br; otsphoto 29 a; papillondream 6 bl; Paul Looyen 35 b, 37 bc; Pete Gallop 18 ar; Pim Leijen 61 al, 61 ac, 61 ar; pirita 31 a; Pookpick Urairat 7 ar; Puhach Andrei 9 al, 9 ar, 9 b; risteski goce 18 bl, 19 bl; Rita Kochmarjova 13 ar, 27 al, 30 al, 63 a; sch_o_n 38; Serg64 39 r; Shin Okamoto 46 l; TFoxFoto 58 ar, 59 ar; Tim_Booth 49 a; TippaPatt 44 b; Tomasz Wrzesien 12 bl; Tsygankova Olga 19 ar; viktori-art 44 ar; Vinit Deekhanu888 51 a; Volodymyr Burdiak 4, 15 bl, 32 br; Wojciech Lisinski 35 a; yevgeniy11 22 ar; Zorandim 17; Zuzule 33

Superstock imageBROKER 55

Contents

Pig

Piglets are sleepy little farm animals.

They snuggle together in deep beds of straw. Their mother feeds them with milk until they are ready to start eating food. Now the baby pigs are called weaners, and they can begin to explore outside!

5

Cat

Cats are hard-working farm animals.

They help the farmer by catching mice and rats. There's plenty of time for playing and sleeping, and cats and kittens can always find a snug corner, or sunny spot, for a snooze!

6

Sheep Dog

Sheep dogs are very smart and they learn fast.

When a sheep dog puppy is just a few months old it must begin its lessons. It will learn how to work on the farm so it can help the farmer. It still has time to sleep and play!

Sheep dogs live with farmers and their families. The farmer teaches them to be obedient so they can help to round up the sheep. Puppies sometimes learn their skills by rounding up ducks or geese first!

Pony

Ponies are usually smaller than horses.

They have a sweet and gentle nature, so children often learn to ride on them. The hair on their head and neck is called a mane. Ponies have longer, fluffier manes than most horses.

13

wild Rabbit

When the sun goes down, wild rabbits come out to play!

They live with their families in burrows, next to fields and under hedges. Baby rabbits nibble at flowers but they also like to eat some of the plants that farmers grow.

Donkey

Donkeys have been used as working animals for thousands of years.

A mother donkey is called a jenny and her baby is a foal. The farmer lets donkeys eat grass in the fields and meadows. In winter, they eat hay and take shelter in barns or stables.

When a foal is born it is skinny, with long legs and ears. Foals can start to play outside when they are just a day old, but the jenny keeps other donkeys away from her baby until it has grown a little stronger. Then it will join the rest of the family.

Llama

This strange-looking animal comes from South America.

Farmers keep llamas so they can use the wool from their fur to make soft, warm cloth. A baby is called a calf or cria. When a mother is scared or wants to protect her baby she might spit!

Chicken

A mother hen lays her eggs in a nest.

She sits on the eggs to keep them warm, so the baby chicks can grow inside. When they are ready to hatch the chicks begin to cheep, and they peck at the eggshell to crack it open.

A chick breaks its egg open and climbs out. It is tiny, soft, and wet. Its feathers soon dry out, and the chick becomes a fluffy ball! It cheeps loudly and quickly finds the mother hen. Soon its brothers and sisters hatch from their eggs too.

Goat

Goats' milk can be used to make cheese.

Baby goats are called kids. They have lots of energy and like to jump and run. Goats can be very noisy animals. Even kids make loud bleats that sound like "baa-baa."

Goats like to explore and climb!
They are curious animals and
they enjoy finding new places
where there are juicy flowers to
eat. Some goats even climb trees
or small buildings and walls.

Horse

A newborn horse is wobbly on its legs!

Just a few hours after being born, a foal can stand up and drink its mother's milk. A boy foal is called a colt and a girl foal is called a filly.

Foals sleep in stables, but they love to go outside where they can run, jump, and explore. Foals play with other foals on the farm, but they always stay close to Mom. She watches over her baby all the time.

Sheep

Lambs are born in spring.

They drink their mom's milk until the new, juicy grass has grown in their fields. Some moms have twins and the farmer helps her feed her babies, using milk in bottles.

Lambs have short, curly fur but as they get older their fur grows long and woolly. Farmers give them a haircut so they don't get too hot! Little lambs love to run and play on the farm.

Turkey

Turkeys come running when the farmer calls.

They spend the day exploring the farm, until they are called to come to the coop, where they sleep. In the wild, turkeys sleep in trees. Young turkeys are called poults and they snuggle up together to keep warm.

39

Sheep-pig

These pigs have curly hair like sheep!

They come from a country called Hungary, where farmers feed them with potatoes and pumpkins. Piglets have stripes, like their wild boar cousins, but it soon grows curly and pale.

JerSey Cow

Gentle Jersey cows are wonderful mothers.

They feed their calves with milk until the babies are old enough to eat grain or grass. Calves live with their families in big groups called herds.

43

Jerseys are shy cows, but they love being stroked, patted, and brushed. Most of all, they like to have their backs scratched! Jersey calves are curious and friendly baby animals.

Alpaca

Alpacas are a type of llama, but they have shorter ears and furrier faces.

Most alpacas can hum, and mothers often hum to let their calves know they are nearby. The calves stay with their mothers until they are at least six months old.

Guinea Fowl

A guinea fowl family scuttles through the grass.

As they run, they whistle and chirp. The chicks look for bugs to eat, and scratch at the ground to find tasty worms and beetles. A guinea hen lays her eggs in the spring, when the weather begins to get warm.

Duck

Ducklings love to swim!

At night, they live inside a barn but in the daytime they like to go outside to explore and visit the farmyard pond. Their webbed feet are perfect for paddling through the water.

A mother duck can lay more than ten eggs in her nest. When they hatch, the ducklings follow their Mom everywhere and they cheep if they can't find her. She quacks back at them!

54

Ostrich

When these little chicks grow up they will be huge!

Ostriches lay the biggest eggs, and are the tallest birds in the world. Farmers often invite visitors to come and watch their amazing birds as they peck, scratch, and nibble in the field.

Pot-bellied Pig

These little piglets eat almost anything!

Pot-bellied pigs come from a country called Vietnam,
but they are now popular pets as well as farm animals.
They like to wallow in mud when the weather is hot
to keep their skin cool. A pig's feet are called trotters
and its nose is called a snout.

Texas Longhorn Cow

These cute calves will grow huge horns, like Mom!

They can be any color, but most Texas Longhorns are red and white. They are smart and gentle cows. Texas Longhorns are also tough animals that don't mind when the weather turns hot and dry.

Goose

Baby geese are called goslings.

They stay in a warm barn until they are a few weeks old. When they go outside they follow Mom everywhere. They like it best when she takes them to a pond for a swim!

Farm Friends

A farm is a place where many animals live.

Some of the baby animals become good friends. They have fun playing or exploring—but the best friends just enjoy spending time together.

63